TOWARDS THE LIGHT

PRINCESS KARADJA

TOWARDS THE LIGHT

Teachings of The Order of Christian Mystics
The "Curtiss Books" freely available at
www.orderofchristianmystics.co.za

1. The Voice of Isis
2. The Message of Aquaria
3. The Inner Radiance
4. Realms of the Living Dead
5. Coming World Changes
6. The Key to the Universe
7. The Key of Destiny
8. Letters from the Teacher Volume I
9. Letters from the Teacher Volume II
10. The Truth about Evolution and the Bible
11. The Philosophy of War
12. Personal Survival
13. The Pattern Life
14. Four-Fold Health
15. Vitamins
16. Why Are We Here?
17. Reincarnation
18. For Young Souls
19. Gems of Mysticism
20. The Temple of Silence
21. The Divine Mother
22. The Soundless Sound
23. The Mystic Life
24. The Love of Rabiacca
25. Potent Prayers

Supporting Volumes

26. The Seventh Seal
27. Towards the Light

TOWARDS THE LIGHT

A MYSTIC POEM

BY
PRINCESS MARY LOUISE KARADJA

2014 EDITION

REPUBLISHED FOR THE ORDER BY
MOUNT LINDEN PUBLISHING
JOHANNESBURG, SOUTH AFRICA
ISBN: 978-1-920483-09-1

"Ministers of Christ and Stewards of the Mysteries of God."
1 Corinthians 4 vs. 1

COPYRIGHT 2014

BY
MOUNT LINDEN PUBLISHING

First Published in 1908

May be used for non-commercial, personal, research and educational use.
ALL RIGHTS RESERVED

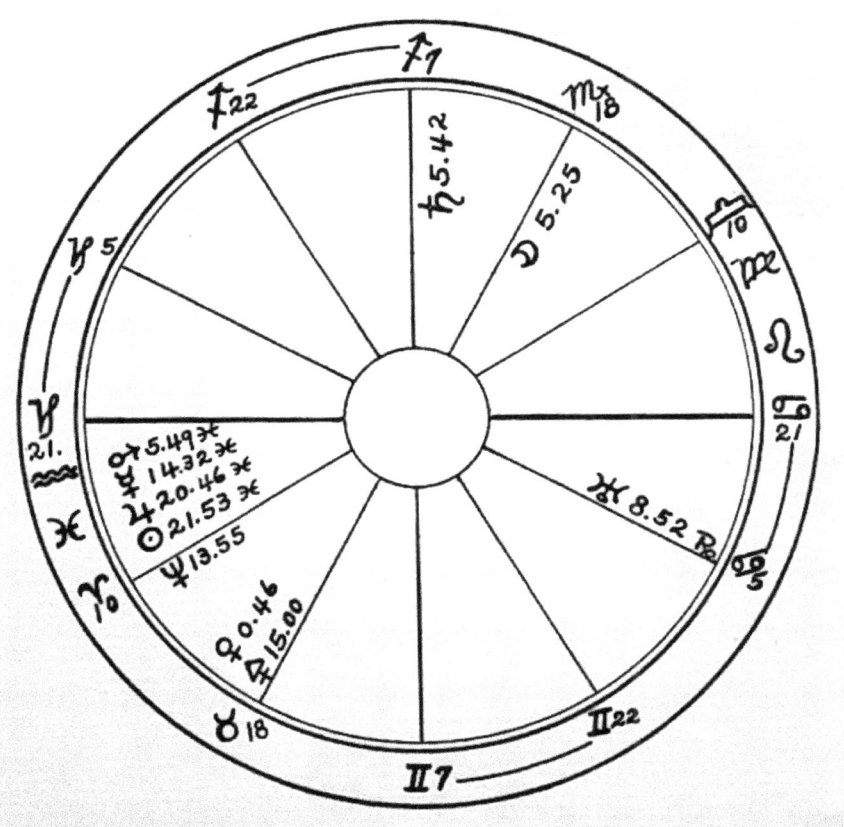

Horoscope of H. H. Princess Karadja
Born March 12, 1868, 5 a. m., Stockholm, Sweden

TABLE OF CONTENTS

CHAPTER   PAGE

    Foreword. ix

    Note by the Author. xvi

    Preface by the Author. xviii

    Towards the Light. 1

FOREWORD

By Dr. W.M. Davidson

It gives me great pleasure to present, to American readers, this unique mystic poem, received by Her Highness, the Princess Karadja of Sweden, in a psychical telepathic state from a discarnate, so-called "dead" man who had committed suicide.

This poem very graphically and dramatically describes the typical after-death sufferings of one who is so misguided as to wantonly throw away the precious gift of life by self-destruction; it most illuminatingly describes the discomforts and inconveniences of the earth-bound state, commonly known as "hell"; it reveals, most suggestively, the way of redemption and liberation for the human soul from these lower states of bondage and, moreover, discloses the ever-present ness of the Angel Kingdom and the Glorious Benediction which These Ministrants of the Laws of God eternally pour down on humankind in its ascent to the Higher Realms of Spirit.

For those who, with Shakespeare, are inclined to regard the grave as "that bourne from which no traveler e'er returns" we would direct attention to three great sources of evidence that there is indeed a life after death. Firstly there are the vast and well authenticated evidences presented by both the English and by the American Societies for Psychical Research—evidences derived from sources which, in the main, are quite without pre-conception or bias for the simple reason that many of them are the experiences which have been thrust upon people who have little or no interest in the question of survival.

Secondly, there is the vast and ever-growing library of literature of communications received from the dead by people in all walks of life, such as Sir Oliver Lodge's communications from his dead son Raymond, Lady Glencommer's messages from her son, the strikingly veridical communications received by Judge Dahlberg from his "dead" son, and a host of others too numerous to mention, the most authentic and verifiable of which I deal with in my lectures on the "After Death."

Thirdly, there are the scientific investigations by means of trained clairvoyance carried out by a number of occult students, and these, collectively, constitute a body of evidence not to be lightly despised—such writers as the late Dr. Annie Besant, the late C. W. Leadbeater, (probably one of the greatest seers of modern times), Mr. Geoffrey Hodson, the late Dr. Rudolph Steiner of Germany, Max Heindel of America, and many other less well known investigators.

This question of communication with the so-called dead is a matter of vast ethical import, for the scientific demonstration of the persistence of consciousness after so-called death is one which science must, sooner or later, frankly face. To the world at large it means also much, for to the sorrowing and bereaved it brings comfort and solace—the realization that death is but the portal to a new and greater life.

Here it might be well that I should relate, in Her Highness's own words, the origin of this mystic poem: "The poem that I now publish was composed under strange circumstances. On midsummernight, 1899, I was alone in the Chapel at Bovigney Castle (her Belgian home) praying on the tomb of my husband and eldest son, when I suddenly heard a voice whisper, "Fetch pen and paper." I obeyed. My hand drew automatically a Sun and wrote the words "Mot Ljuset" (Swedish for "Towards the Light") without any help of my personal will. When I took the pen in my hand I had no idea about what I was going to write, but nevertheless I wrote fluently hundreds of verses. I must have become entranced. It seemed to me that the temperature fell quickly. I felt chilled, although the summer heat was oppressive. My soul was detached; all my senses were sharpened and acquired an extraordinary lucidity; I was so distinctly conscious of the spirit voices that it was almost as if I had written their dictation. Anyone who reads this poem might believe it to be the result of long religious meditation, but such is not the case. The soul whose evolution is here narrated was an utter stranger to me. Most of the thoughts contained in this poem were not mine five minutes before I wrote them down. Where then did they come from? No thoroughly satisfactory answer can be given to that question. Telepathy is the only possible solution of such phenomena. Telepathy must take place in the same way that radio communication now takes place. This little known psychical force will undoubtedly be mastered in the future. People will then be able to communicate with their discarnate friends. A hundred years ago the idea that two people might communicate with each other by means of a wire was considered preposterous. The thought of communication without a wire utterly undreamed of. Yet today these are accomplished facts and only steps toward the communication of minds directly.

I shall therefore not be in the least surprised if my statement concerning the origin of this poem be doubted, contradicted or denied; but I have decided to endure, with resignation, the annoyances to which I may consequently expose myself. No one who is not willing to endure personal inconvenience for the sake of truth is worthy of bearing witness of eternal verities."

This poem has been translated from the original Swedish into seven languages and has aroused great interest in all parts of the world.

Occult students will not be surprised to know that this psychical experience was the beginning of great spiritual illumination which has been continuously flowing into the consciousness of Her Highness for the last twenty years. It has been my privilege to be the recipient of some of these manuscripts, many of which constitute distinct contributions to the mysteries of Occultism, and which, I trust, it will be found possible to publish in the near future.

Readers who are familiar with the truths of Astrology will doubtlessly be interested in the Horoscope of H. H. the Princess Karadja, which I calculated for her many years ago, and so I take pleasure in presenting it along with this most enthralling poem. The significance of the position of the Moon, the typifier of the psychical side of nature, in the eighth mansion, the House of Death, will be readily comprehended by students of the occult. Her Highness subsequently experienced many psychical revelations and thus gained a knowledge of her former lives upon earth. The eighth house has especial dominion over the "dream state" of consciousness and it is quite surprising how many people who have the Moon in a water sign in this House experience highly premonitional dreams, and who, furthermore, in this state, gain memories of former incarnations.

I am greatly indebted to Her Highness for permission, so graciously granted, to present this poem as the first of a series of brochures dealing with various phases of the Ancient Wisdom.

That it may help to dispel the darkness and shed some vital light upon the great problems which beset humanity is my sincere wish.

W. M. D.

Human Science Research Publishing Co.

Note by the Author

This poem which is now brought to the knowledge of the British and American public was originally written in Swedish. It was published in that language a few years ago and met with extraordinary success. Six large editions were rapidly sold out. German, Dutch, and Danish versions soon appeared. French, Italian, and Russian are to follow.

I have myself undertaken the English translation, but am indebted to several friends for many a valuable hint.

It is no easy task to handle poetry in a foreign tongue. I claim the indulgence of my readers for this first attempt at English blank verse.

PRINCESS KARADJA

BOVIGNY CASTLE,
GOUVY, BELGIUM

Preface by the Author

THE poem that I now publish was composed under strange circumstances.

On midsummer night, 1899, I was alone in the chapel at Bovigny Castle, praying on the tomb of my husband and eldest son, when I suddenly heard a voice whisper: "Fetch pen and paper."

I obeyed. My hand drew automatically a sun, and wrote the words "Mot Ljuset" ("Towards the Light") without help of my personal will. When I took the pen in my hand, I had no idea about what I was going to write, but nevertheless I wrote fluently hundreds of verses. I must have become entranced. . . . It seemed to me that the temperature fell quickly. . . . I felt chilled, although the summer heat was oppressive. My soul was detached, all my senses were sharpened and acquired an extraordinary lucidity. I was so distinctly conscious of the spirit voices that it was almost as if I had written under dictation.

Everybody who reads this poem might probably believe it to be the result of long religious meditation, but such is not the case.

The soul whose evolution is narrated was an utter stranger to me. Most of the thoughts contained in this poem were not mine five minutes before I wrote them down.

WHERE DID THEY COME FROM?

No satisfactory answer can be given to that question. Telepathy is the only possible explanation of such phenomena. Telepathy—transmission of thought—must take place in some way similar to wireless telegraphy.

Vibrations of thought flash through the ether as well as electric waves. This now little-known psychic force will probably be mastered in the future. Living men will then, without difficulty, be able to communicate with their disembodied friends. Fifty years ago the idea that two people might exchange thoughts at a distance of a hundred miles, by telephone, would have been considered preposterous. For my part I am absolutely convinced that free intercourse between liberated spirits and incarnated souls is simply a question of time.

In every period of history each new idea has to fight its way. Most people consider everything that they have not personally experienced to be more or less incredible. I shall therefore not be in the least surprised if my statement concerning the origin of this poem is doubted, contradicted, or ridiculed; but I have decided to endure with resignation the annoyances to which I may consequently expose myself.

Nobody who is not willing to endure personal inconvenience for the sake of truth is worthy to bear witness of eternal verities.

Towards the Light

OH! Watcher in the silent hours of night,
Art thou prepared to greet thy noiseless guests,
The messengers from distant spirit worlds?
On rapid wings they now are speeding hither.
They float around thee; canst thou not perceive them?
Soon shall thy spirit's eye discern their forms.
Hark, child of earth! A chime of silver bells
Descends to thee from starry worlds above,
While gentle fragrances enchant thy sense.
The darkness dies. . . . A radiant light appears.
Behold the ambient flame encircling thee,
That flame of living light—it is my soul!

My voice now whispers gently in thine ear:
I too was once a mortal such as thou.
I am not dead, although my dust has lain
Deep in the silent tomb for many years.
I am not dead! My spirit still is living,
Serene and strong, robed in immortal garb.

I will to thee my earthly life unfold,
Then shalt thou comprehend thy future fate,
For I shall show thee all the path I trod
From earthly darkness to the spheres of light.
Thou art a tool, chosen by Higher Powers,
To tell the world what thou shalt here behold.
The gift of words is thine; thou shalt express
My mighty thought, which dominates thy mind.
Unknown to thee I hither led thy steps;
Thy destiny I welded link by link.
My hand, oh woman! chiselled out thy soul:
Resist thy Guide no more! Submit in peace!
No blessed crop can grow on untilled ground;
Deep furrows have been driven in thy heart,
And now at last I sow: mine hour has come!
May God in mercy overshadow us!
I lift thy soul up to the source of Light;
Help others as I now am helping thee.
Write down the message that I bring tonight
With humble thanks because thy hand was chosen!
"Who art thou?"—dost thou ask.—I am a sinner,
Who through repentance has atoned his crimes.

My name on earth is utterly forgotten;
My race is swept away from off its face.

———

I WAS a man who once had rich possessions;
Alas! A sorry use I made of all. . . .
No gentle memories of loving deeds
Survived me in the dismal hour of death.
Yet once I did possess a thousand treasures—
Rank, beauty, health and riches—all were mine.
Men envied me as fortune's petted child.
I deemed myself created to enjoy,
And carefully fulfilled that pleasant mission.
No broken sob could reach my deadened ear,
Nor raise an echo in my empty heart,
Where on a throne of ice my spirit dwelt,
Adoring as supreme Divinity,
As centre of the world, as Lord and God
The only being whom I loved—*Myself!*

But years rolled on. . . . ever the well-known round!
Earth had no pleasure left for me to taste.
I was so weary that life's pageant palled,
And duller, greyer, grew the lengthening days.

My selfish soul was filled with blank despair.
I grew to hate the joys that could not still
My craving after *something* I had missed,
A precious *something* I had failed to win.
What might it be, I knew not—only this:
Without it life was wasted, drear and void.

AT last when I had emptied to the dregs
Life's pleasure-cup, I longed for dreamless sleep.
The chill embrace of death would cool my brain....
Rest! Rest! Eternal rest—oh, priceless boon!
I had no terror of the starless night,
And scorned the thought of coming Judgment Day.
Annihilation seemed to me elysian,
for I was weary—weary unto death.
But in farewell I first would summon round me
All that in former days had charmed me most:
Wine, women, music, light and fragrant flowers—
And so surrounded I would breathe my last.

IT was a merry night and I the gayest,
Because Life's dreary farce so soon would end.

Towards the Light

'T was my last pride to smilingly approach,
Without a trace of fear, my yawning tomb.

The flickering lights burned low; the flowers
 drooped;
The hour grew late; my noisy friends had gone.
One guest remained—I was alone with Death
Whom I had dared to summon to my feast.

  * * * * * *
  * * * * * *

A flash—a shot—then deepest silence reigned.
One thrill of anguish quivered through my frame—
Then all was still! A sense of dreary numbness
Crept slowly, surely over all my limbs.
Around me deepest night. . . . Yea. . . . ebon
 darkness.
If death had come why did it fail to bring
The blessed sleep for which I yearned so long?
When would oblivion sweep away the past?
Why this delay? At last a dawning fear
Shook me that something would *begin*—but what?
I waited thus with panic-stricken soul. . . .

Death I had courted to escape my thoughts;
I had destroyed myself; I must be dead!
I felt my body growing stiff and cold;
The heart had ceased to beat, the pulse stood still.
I was a corpse—mere matter—nothing more,
A thing which surely was bereft of sense—
Yet—after death—how could my body think?
I was aghast, for now at last I knew
That I had failed to murder all in me,
One part was left—*my thought was still alive!*

*   *   *   *   *   *

NO mortal words can ever paint the terror
That seized me when I grasped that awful fact.
My senses seemed to whirl in stormy chaos—
What would my future be? When should I know?
The night was dark; nowhere a ray of light. . . .
And I must wait. . . . For what? I dared not guess.
Was it eternity—was it an hour
That I endured this torture of suspense?
I cannot tell! It seemed a thousand years,
To be alive against my will! What doom
For me, who hoped the grave to be the end!

Could there be truth, then, in the Devil's creed
Of an avenging God, who, merciless,
Condemns all sinners to eternal hell?
If so, I meant to bravely meet my Judge,
And to receive erect the cruel sentence.
I courage felt to calmly all endure—
If but the torture of suspense might end.
Still time went on.... In vain I claimed my doom.
No Judge appeared! A cry of keen distress
Broke forth at last, deep from my frenzied heart;
I clamoured wildly: "Oh, have mercy, Lord!"
A voice at once replied from out the gloom:
"What is thy wish? What favour dost thou claim
From God, whom thou hast all thy life denied?"
I murmured humbly: "Lord, a ray of Light!"

*   *   *   *   *   *

AT once a flash of Radiance fell on me,
And I beheld myself! Oh, bitter shame!
Most ghastly is that moment for the man
Who lived in utter darkness here on earth.
Pray for the blind, that they may not despair
When after death at last their opened eye

Shrinks from the sight which they are forced to see,
A human heart in hideous nakedness!
The angels of the Lord behold it trembling,
And turn away at once their shuddering glance.
In abject shame the soul attempts to hide,
And, full of anguish, begs for solitude.
God grants that grace. The soul is left alone—
Alone with all the shadows of the past.
I saw my earthly life glide past in vision. . . .
Scene after scene, forgotten long ago.
How blind—insanely blind, had I not been!
The sight of all my crimes confounded me.
They crushed my spirit with their leaden weight. . . .
At last I whispered: "Punish me, oh Lord!"
The voice replied: "God claims no penalty.
Sin punishes itself. Each evil seed
Allowed to grow in wanton liberty
Must bear its bitter crop of pain and woe.
The angels of the Lord no anger feel
At human crime; they see its fruit and mourn.
Unhappy spirit, thou hast asked thy sentence!
Learn, then, that long ago thy fate was sealed.
'There where thy treasure is, thy heart will be.'

Thus spake the Christ. These words contain thy
  doom.
Each man has something which he dearest holds—
His God,—a fellow creature, or himself.
On earth he is at liberty to choose
A treasure to be kept eternally.
The soul can after death no more abandon
What during life it found most fit to love.
What was thy treasure? Hapless fool—behold it!"

A FLOOD of light streamed down and I perceived
A lifeless body stretched upon the floor
Amidst a pool of blood. It was my corpse.
"Behold thy treasure! Thou canst claim no other.
Thou art compelled to keep thy cherished God.
Thou mad'st an idol of a lump of clay,—
No more to leave it is thy awful doom."
"No, no!" I shrieked, "I will not thus be fettered!
Ah! Loose me from the body I destroyed!
I love no more this thing. I hate to see it.
Oh, set me free! In mercy break my chains!"
"Hark! Thou hast entered spirit life unbidden;
No room with us was yet prepared for thee.
The threshold of Eternity no man

May cross before his final hour has struck.
The plans of God no mortal ever altered:
He is the Master over Life and Death.
There is a lesson all on earth must learn
And none may slip away, the task undone;
Nor lightly fling the human garb aside,
Until the soul is fit to leave its dwelling.
Woe to the man who scorns the gift of life,
Who, greatly daring Heaven, would extinguish
The spark Divine, which burns within his soul!
The deed is vain, he only makes more sure
The fate he has created by his acts.
The sacred tie, uniting soul and body,
Is only severed at the Lord's Command.
The will of thy Creator links thy spirit
Still for a time to this poor clay. . . . Submit!
Learn to abide in patience — captive soul —
The day when liberty shall dawn for thee."
"So hope remains? My punishment will end?
I am not chained for all eternity?"
I cried aloud, all thrilled with gratitude.
The angel answered: "Every pain will end.
One sin alone can never be forgiven,
The sin of pride that does not wish for grace,

For then the spirit dooms itself to darkness.
God's arms are ever open. Every soul
That struggles bravely upwards finds the Light.
Though far the Goal—yet it is reached at last!"
I murmured low: "Most merciful thou art.
Oh, glorious angel, let me know thy name."
"Canst thou not guess it? Often I approached
Thy stony heart and strove to gain admittance,
But was repelled as soon as I drew near.
I am the mournful angel men call Grief!
The Lord of Mercy sends me down to earth
To show the way, which leads men up to Him.
I sow in sinful hearts contrition's seed,
Then buds humility from burning shame.
The yearning soul strives hard to leave the mire;
Though weak and trembling still it bravely seeks
To climb the thorny path to which I point.
Then hasten to his aid the Radiant Host,
Who, in the name of Christ, work deeds of love.
Their gentle hands cannot remove all pain,
But they give strength to bear the heavy cross.
They fill the weary soul with hope and courage,
And whisper promises of coming bliss.
The pilgrim soon is taught to fix his gaze

Above the darkness of this present world,
Up to the distant home where all is peace.
For thee there still remains thy crown to earn
Of Faith and Hope and Charity entwined.
These thou must tend and nourish in thy heart,
But first the arduous task of 'Patience' learn!"

———————

*H*OW desolate and cold the graveyard seemed!
My only home in dismal winter-nights
If I had better used the gift of life
Preparing me a nest in faithful hearts,
My frozen soul might now have been their guest,
And found relief and warmth at friendly hearths.
Alas! On earth was none of human kind
Whose grief attracted with magnetic power
My wretched soul, by all alive forgotten.
I was alone in solitary gloom,
The one companion left—my lifeless frame.
Despairingly I searched a thousand graves
In hope to find another living soul
Chained to the empty forms that mouldered here
Beneath the snow. . . . Alas! It was in vain!
Each soul had left the worn-out shell of dust

In former days the object of its pride.
Each one had gladly flown. I—I alone
Was still a captive in this place of dread,
Indissolubly fettered to my corpse.
No thing on earth e'er filled me with such loathing!
My ghastly treasure! . . . . With intense disgust
Day after day I watched its slow decay.
Sometimes the broken eyes would seem to weep
As though, attempting to express my grief,
They fain would bring me the relief of tears. . . .

*O*NE night I wandered round the dreary grounds
And reached the gate. Then in the dismal darkness
I heard a broken sob, a feeble wailing.
Who could it be? Who broke the ghastly silence?
A living being? If so—why came he here?
It was a child, a small deserted child,
Left here to perish in the winter snow.
I felt compassion for the tiny waif
Who softly sobbed himself to sleep forever,
And anger 'gainst the mother who could leave
Her child alone to meet a frozen death.
What punishment too great for such a sin?

What could atone for such a cruel deed?
In righteous wrath I cried: "Accurst be she
Who has abandoned this defenceless child!"
Like a clap of thunder rang the answer forth:
"Man, who art thou, who darest thus call down
The holy wrath of God upon thy sister?
The sinner thou hast recklessly condemned
Thou shalt behold! Repent thy malediction!
Leave to thy God, the Strong Avenger's hands
The care of vindicating martyr's blood!"

*B*ESIDE me stood an angel. Sad and stern
I found his look, which seemed to pierce my soul.
He grasped the hand I tremblingly outstretched,
Then, swift as thought, he swept away with me.
He took me to the city where I lived
In former days. We reached a den of vice,
Where during life I was a constant guest.
At his command I entered it again. . . .
How weird, how strange appeared the house of sin!
Aghast, I saw among the shameless crowd
Unnoticed guests from silent spirit-worlds
Stand dark and threat'ning close behind the living.

I saw how evil souls with deadly hate
Urge fallen men to ever darker deeds;
I saw God's angels struggling hard to save
The sparks of virtue, not extinguished yet.
This noisy palace was a battlefield,
Where little recked the mortals that their fate
Hung on the silent fight 'twixt light and darkness.
But many gloomy spirits, too, I marked,
Who did not fight, but wandered round the place
In dismal watchfulness and dumb despair.
These were the souls, who once had thriven there.
Mortals, who spend their lives in wanton revels,
Mourn bitterly, when solemn death appears,
And sternly summons them to leave this world.
They strive against their lot. . . . They fain would linger
Still on this earth, whose vilest pleasures
Emprison after death their hapless souls.
They have no strength to rend the loathsome fetters,
That vice has forged. Earth's joys they still remember. . . .
Alas, poor slaves! They love and miss them yet.
Their evil lusts remain and torture them
Since they no longer can be satisfied.

Thus they remain until desire is dead,
Compelled to watch the sins of living men.
At length they loathe the very sight of vice.
Then slowly they forget their low delights:
Unclean remembrances are swept away. . . .
The soul begins to long for purer air
And lifts its weary glance from dismal earth.
Till lo! It sees a ray of distant heaven
And stretches unaccustomed arms in prayer. . . .
The heavy chains slip off: the soul is free!
Magnetic force attracts it up to God.
When no regrets enchain the soul to earth
Then it is lifted up by ardent longing
To radiant spheres, that it cannot approach
Until it learns that Death means—Liberty.

I NOTICED then a spirit standing by,
With wistful gaze intently bent on me.
How well I knew the form. . . . It was my mother!
I flew to greet her with a cry of joy,
But she drew back avoiding my embrace.
On earth my mother's arms were never closed
Against the son she tenderly adored.
Now—mournfully she pointed to the crowd

Surrounding us.... With burning shame I cried:
"Oh, Mother! Mother! Have I brought you here?"
She bowed her head in silent, tearless sorrow....
Then brokenly she whispered: "Oh, my son!
You were my idol—dearer than my God,
Who granted me the gift of motherhood.
Enthralled by trammels of an earthly love,
No soul can rise. The tie must first be broken—
The clay we worship from its altar flung.
When death approached, I yearned to stay with you.
I had my wish! I was no longer free.
My love had grown a chain attaching me
Close to your side. Invisible I stood
And read within your heart your guilty thoughts—
I followed you with horror to this place....
My son! My son! You were my pride and joy,
But now my head is bent in shame for you.
You added grievous burden to my cross
By dragging me with you to degradation."

I STOOD amazed and overcome with grief:
"Oh! Mother! Dearest mother—pardon me!
I did not know.... Oh! had I only guessed
That your pure eyes could see my darkest deeds,

My evil angel should not have prevailed.
Nay, I had fought him then with might and main.
No man on earth can surely be so fallen,
That he would plunge in vice, if but he knew
His mother's eyes could follow him. . . . Each one
Would shudder at the thought that the departed,
Dear to his heart, was thus compelled to be
A silent witness to his hidden sins!
Atrocious is my doom! Yet—well deserved. . . .
But you! What crime is yours? Your love for me?
Are mothers punished for their deep devotion?
Unjust is He, who such a verdict passed."
The shade of holy wrath, which long had darkened
My mother's tender features, vanished now.
She gently smiled: "Do not so quickly judge
The sacred laws, you fail to understand.
If keener pain is measured out to me
Than I deserve—I suffer not in vain!
It is for your dear sake. . . . I murmur not.
One day, my grief shall be your gain, my child.
When once you truly grasp the love of Christ,
Who suffered meek a thousand pangs for us,
Then at the mem'ry of your mother's grief
You will adore the mercy of the Lord."

"You love me still—although you now have gazed
Into the deep abyss, down which I fell?"
I cried, all trembling with surprise and joy.

THEN in a whisper soft the answer came:
"I love you still—but now with tender pity.
My blind devotion helped to ruin you.
No mortal man is fit to be adored;
I worship you no more! My broken idol
Has lost the power to enthral my heart.
Woe unto me! . . . . I knew not, in my blindness,
That women harm the men they long to serve
By giving all and claiming nothing. Love
Must be the recompense of noble strife;
A price to victory—then it is precious!
The love a man deserves—he values high;
The love unearned, despises wantonly.
Once I was weak—the slave of my own heart;
Now I am strong: the ruler of my love.
It has no more the power to hold me down;
Strength from above is granted it—to raise!"
"Oh, mother dear! Do not abandon me!
I am unworthy of your love"—I cried.
"But do not leave me, hopeless and alone!

You have your liberty: I still am chained. . . .
Remain with me, though you at last are free!"
She answered gently: "Such a sacrifice
Would bring no benefit to you, my son.
My mother-heart would gladly share your woe
If, by the sharing, I might rend your bonds.
Alas! Each spirit has to fight alone
The strenuous battle with the lower self.
No other back than ours may bear our load;
No human aid can drag for us our cross.
The only help I can bestow — is prayer.
Allow no hopeless sorrows to consume you,
Because I am compelled to leave your side.
My yearning lifts me upward: you will follow
When you have learned to meekly bear your fate.
Be brave! For every victory you gain
You will receive sweet comfort from above."

*M*Y mother vanished. I was left alone. . . .
No friend in all this crowd! I felt myself
Abandoned, lost and utterly forlorn,
My heart was filled with bitterness intense.
Then to the angel at my side I turned:
"Behold! Oh Lord! Even my mother shuns me. . . .

Let me return unto my lonely grave!
I will not linger in this noisy crowd:
Abhorrent to me is the sight of sin,
I suffered less in my dark solitude."
"Remember thy companion at thy grave,"
The angel gently said. "Fulfil thy mission!
The child is still alive. Go—find its mother
And crush her with thy righteous malediction!
Behold the woman in that corner crouching. . . .
Draw near! 'Tis she—go and observe her well."

*I*N silence I reluctantly obeyed.
The pangs of grief had cooled my earlier wrath;
Revengeful thoughts within me long had died.
What could I have to do with that poor creature
Her shocking sin was no concern of mine.
I could not clearly see the woman's face,
For she had hidden it with both her hands,
And 'gainst the table rested wearily.
Exhausted, desperate, she seemed to be
A wounded animal that yearns to die. . . .
She could not laugh, as others of her trade,
Nor weep. . . . The fountain of her tears had dried.
I watched the hapless creature till my heart

Grew soft to her. The angel whispered low:
"This is the woman, thou hast dared to curse!
Remembrance of her child now tortures her. . . .
Behold her grief! What pang hast thou to add
To crush more utterly that broken heart?
Why art thou silent? Dost thou fear to judge
The fallen sister, who before thee stands?
God's justice she shall not confront alone:
There is a man whose sin is greater still.
That babe a father had! It was his duty
To give protection unto child and mother.
He cast them both aside! This coward deed
For vengeance cries to heaven, though on earth
Such acts are not condemned by human laws.
God made man strong that he might help the weak
Whom now he ruins, careless of remorse.
Behold this woman here, so deeply sunken!
There was a time when she was sweet and pure;
Her only treasure—her chaste innocence—
She, thoughtless, gave away with lavish hands.
The man she loved and trusted took the gift
And in return gave lifelong shame and grief.
He needed not her love. . . . An idle hour
It gratified a passing whim—no more!

Cold scorn and mockery assailed her steps
Wherever with her nameless child she went.
Each door was closed.... This one alone was open;
So in despair the little one she left.
Who for this crime should justly bear the blame?"
Impulsively I cried: "The heartless father!
He murdered both the mother and the child.
So base a scoundrel is not fit to live!"
The angel murmured: "Look at her once more
And beg thy God to be a lenient Judge!"

I LOOKED—and looked again—with wonder filled....
And suddenly it seemed to me I knew her....
Her bended form familiar was to me.
I sought 'mid half forgotten memories:
I must have known her—surely, ah! But where?
She raised her face: I saw the pallid features....
Oh God! 'twas she—the happy, playful child,
Whose rosy lips—alas—had tempted me.
I recognised the spot beneath the curls,
Where I had kissed her last with languid lips.
I sank together with a shuddering cry.
The angel sternly said: "Thou art the man!

The helpless infant, flung away to perish,
Whom thou hast deigned to pity—is thy son.
The tiny victim waits.... Come, watch him die!"

ONCE more I stood beside the lonely spot,
Where—on his bed of snow—the boy was resting.
He was alive as yet, although the breathing
Could scarcely be perceived, so faint it was.
I bent despairing o'er the prostrate form
And cried aloud in bitter helplessness:
"Oh, could I purchase with a thousand pangs
One hour of life—that life I once disdained,
How quickly I would fly to summon help.
My hapless child, thou wouldst not perish thus!"
My sigh no echo raised.... It died unheard.
The howling gale alone gave me response
By heaping higher drifts of glitt'ring snow
All round that fragile wreck of human life.
The child would perish if no help arrived....
No *hope* was possible—yet still I hoped!
It could not—should not be.... I must prevent
My crime from reaping such a bitter harvest.
Alas! I had no power to help. I felt

My utter nothingness. My very soul
Rose up to God in ardent supplication.
In that dark hour of anguish *faith* was born—
Faith in the mighty Lord, whose hand can snatch
Away from death its victims. I attempted
To lift my being on the wings of prayer,
Humbly imploring God to spare my child.
I then perceived a multitude of angels;
Their silver voices chanted—"Pray as we:
Thy will be done in heaven and on earth,
Oh God of love, forever and forever!"
I sank again down from the dazzling worlds
To which my ardent thought had tried to soar;
Half blinded by the glories there perceived
I never dared to stammer forth my prayer.
How dismal, cold and dark the earth appeared.
Poor child! Why had I wished to chain him there?
No! No! I ought no longer to prevent
His pure, white soul from taking instant flight
Straight to the arms of Christ—the children's friend.
A martyr's crown waits those who meekly suffer
For others' guilt. . . . My son had won that crown.
"Ah! What is this? Whence comes this wondrous light

Which now illuminates the night with brilliance?
It emanates from me! "I saw a flame,
Which issued from my icy heart—'t was *love*.
That spark from heaven, kindled by my child,
Was fed with burning fuel of repentance.
All thrilled with joy, I felt a stream of warmth,
Of radiant light, all through my being glow.
At last I knew how sweet it is to love,
And felt most grateful to have learned that lesson.

THE end drew near.... A snow-white childish soul
Emerged from out its broken fragile shell;
And I drew back, not daring to approach,
Lest he in terror should recoil from me,
And shun the father who had given him
The wretched gift of life, —and nothing else.
The child was gazing out.... He felt alone
There on the threshold of that unknown world
To which he had been summoned. Would he still
No father find, with sheltering arms outstretched?
On earth his greeting was a mother's tears....
Though innocent, he was the child of shame.
He had been born.... That was his only crime!

Was not that crime by death atoned in full?
Now that to spirit life he had returned,
Was there no father who his duty knew?
He looked around and then perceived at last
The flame, which from my soul leapt forth to meet him:
"I missed thee, whom I never knew on earth!"
He whispered, nestling in my hungry arms—
"Oh father, where thou stayest, let me stay!"
"No! No! Around me all is cold and dreary. . . .
Poor child, I will not share with thee my woe.
My crime against thee would still more oppress me
If I delayed thy luminous ascent.
Look up! Behold the thousand stars of heaven:
Thy home is there! Spread out thy snowy wings!
I love thee. Gladly will I now renounce
The joy thy presence would have given me.
Farewell, we soon shall meet. I follow thee,
When in His mercy, God my pardon seals."
The child then cried: "See, see thy chain is broken!
Oh father! Thou art free! What blessed joy. . . .
Now, hand in hand to heaven we can rise
We two—together—always. God is good!"

WHAT glorious bliss it was at last to fly
Away from cloudy earth in liberty
And to approach the sun, whose golden rays
Surrounded us with roseate brilliancy.
Divinely fair is the eternal dawn,
Which greets the first ascension of the soul.
Its wondrous splendour mirrors faintly forth
The great Creator's own magnificence.
Praise, glory and thanksgiving unto God,
Who made the sun—an emblem of Himself.
The human eye cannot endure its radiance;
When spirits lift their glance to it they tremble
And reverently bend in adoration
Of that sun's origin, the Source of Life.
Man can by virtue of his thoughts create
A tiny world of beauty for himself.
The thoughts of God gave birth to lustrous heavens;
The stars are a reflection of His glory.
Life, Love and Light compose the Trinity.
A myriad sparks proceeded from that source.
Each spark must grow till it becomes a flame,
Which through Eternity will not be quenched.
How is the soul to grow? Through sorrow only,
For grief makes man grow greater than himself.

Affliction winnows tares from out the wheat. . . .
The wheat grows up. . . . It is the crop of God.
Behold the drops of rain, which fall from heaven;
They mingle briefly with the dust of earth,
Until the sun recalls them from the clay,
And lifts each sparkling drop up to the skies.
So shall at last each wand'ring soul return
Unto the Source of Life from which it flowed,
There to enjoy communion with the Christ
And merge in perfect unison with God.
There is no Paradise of idle rest,
Where blessed spirits dwell in aimless joy.
The highest goal to which we can aspire
Is to resemble God. To reach that end
We struggle upwards through a million years.
Eternal hope brings us eternal joy:
We paradise create within our breast.

WHEN Sorrow comes to visit human hearts,
That Angel's mission is to sweep the Temple
Where God Himself elects in grace to dwell.
We follow in the mighty steps of Grief
With gentle tread and cool the burning wound;
We kiss away the tear which hides the sky.

Another Angel comes.... His name is PEACE.
He finds in broken hearts a resting place.
To ev'ry spot on earth where prayers rise
We quickly fly and carry them to heaven,
Descending swift with blessing from above.
We watch in patience by the bed of pain
And guide the falt'ring steps of infant souls;
We fill the poet's dreams with wondrous beauty,
And bid him hear a strain of angels' songs.
His silent sobs we melt in harmony....
His highest thought is but a gift from us.
Say! Can there be a fairer paradise?
Can mortals dream a joy exceeding ours?
Like Christ, we always sacrifice ourselves,
Yet keep eternally more than we give.

Now dawn is near.... Thy lamp is burning low!
Thy weary head sinks down in lassitude.
Thy task is done. Our spirit child created!
Fruit of my thought—it has grown up in thee;
In pain brought forth, but yet of love begotten.
The seed he bears within is Life Eternal.

That seed will germinate in bleeding hearts
And ripen to a crop of richest blessing.

   *   *   *   *   *   *

BOVIGNY CHAPEL, BELGIUM.
Midsummernight, 1899.

www.ingramcontent.com/pod-product-compliance
Lightning Source LLC
Chambersburg PA
CBHW060722030426
42337CB00017B/2967